AF481055

Cafe Rouge

The entrance door to 'Cafe Rouge' swings open and Naana walks in with a smile on her face. She says a quick hello to the manager and the waiter and quickly slides into her favorite booth. Naana sets up her laptop and books on the table and orders for her favorite Hot Chocolate drink as she begins work on her computer.

This is an almost everyday routine for Naana, a third year law student. She enjoys the peace and quiet that she finds at the 'Cafe Rouge', a cafe that is situated just two streets from her house, but mainly, she uses the internet service available to the customers at 'Cafe Rouge' to finish off assignments and carry out research work for school projects.

When she's at the cafe, her favorite things to order are hot chocolate drink and cappuccino. She loves so many drinks on the menu, everything tastes amazing. She always wonders how they come up with such delicious drinks.

Soon, it's time to go home. Naana is done with her assignments. She pays her bill, tips the waiter and gets going.

School is about to go on vacation. This season, Naana thinks to herself, she must find work to support herself in getting some extra case law books for study. In her fourth year, she will embark on an internship program in a law firm, but until then, Naana needs to earn some bucks.

Naana decides to go to the manager of 'Cafe Rouge' and apply for a temporal job to help her save up during the vacation. When she approaches the manager, he listens carefully and replies "well why not? That is a brilliant idea, we do need some extra hands around here".

Naana is excited. She heads back to campus for an afternoon lecture on the law of contracts. As she takes notes, Naana realizes how the elements of a contract are evident in our everyday activities.

She recalls the conversation she had with the manager of Cafe Rouge and notes the elements that are capable of being enforceable as a contract. Naana appreciates the lessons she learnt from the lecture so much; she now knows to look out for **Offer** and **Acceptance, Consideration, Capacity, Intention to create legal relations, legality, Certainty** and **Awareness** in order for a contract to be legally binding on both parties. This knowledge will come in handy for when she is set to begin work at Cafe Rouge.

Naana arrives at Cafe Rouge on her usual routine as she sets her laptop and books on the table to begin reading her case laws in preparation for her exams.
She ponders on the elements of a contract in Law.

Offer:
An offer is an expression where one party agrees to enter into a contract with another party for a consideration.

Acceptance:
Acceptance is where one party agrees to he conditions of an offer made.

Consideration:
Consideration refers to the promise made by the party who makes an offer and the performance thereof by the party who accepts the offer.

Capacity:
For a contract to be legally binding, parties to the contract must be legally capable of entering into the contract.

Intention to Create Legal Relations:
Both parties to a contract must have the intention to be legally bound by the terms of the contract.

Naana receives her order for her favorite hot chocolate drink and takes a sip before continuing to ponder on the elements of a contract.

**Legality:**
This refers to whether or not the terms agreed to in the contract is legally enforceable or in accordance with the law.

**Certainty:**
The terms of a contract should not be vague to either party, terms should be clear to both parties.

**Awareness:**
Both parties to a contract must be aware that they are entering into an agreement.

Naana continues reading until her alarm beeps. It's time to head home as she packs up and pays her bill before leaving the cafe.

When school goes on vacation, Naana goes to the manager of Cafe Rouge to sign a legally binding contract to offer her services as a waitress for a period of 6 weeks before school reopens for an agreed wage.

She is set to begin work the next day.

Naana receives training on customer service on her first day. She is a very fast learner and soon she wins the heart of customers with her smiles and how quickly she delivers the orders.

The barista at the cafe; Toby, offers to teach Naana how to make her favorite hot chocolate drink upon request and hands her the recipe;


## HOT CHOCOLATE DRINK

Ingredients:

- 1 tbsp Chocolate sauce
- 1 tbsp Cocoa powder
- 2 tbsp Hot water
- 2 cups Steamed milk
- ¼ cup Shaved chocolate

METHOD:
- Pour 1tbsp of chocolate sauce into a glass
- Add the 1 tbsp cocoa powder
- Add 2 tbsp hot water and stir to dissolve
- Add half of your steamed milk and stir
- Add the rest of the steamed milk without stirring
- Pour shaved chocolate over the hot chocolate drink ad serve

Naana is so excited. She is eager to serve the next customer who orders a hot chocolate drink so that she could prepare it.

On the second day of work, Naana arrives an hour earlier than her shift is scheduled to begin. She is excited about the lesson the barista gave her and requests for another lesson before work begins. Toby the barista is pleased to teach Naana because she makes training very easy. Today you are going to learn how to make **Hot Caramel Macchiato.**

## HOT CARAMEL MACCHIATO

Ingredients:

- 10ml Caramel Sauce
- 10ml Vanilla syrup
- 35ml Espresso
- 1 cup Milk

METHOD:
- In a glass, mix caramel sauce, vanilla and espresso
- Steam milk with the espresso machine to foam
- Pour steamed milk into a glass
- Pour espresso mix into the milk foam
- Design the surface with caramel sauce

Naana loves the taste of this caramel macchiato. She knows she's going to recommend it to customers.

The next day, Toby was off duty. Usually, the cafe serves their special on his off days since there is no replacement for Toby on such days. Cafe Rouge is a small place with a limited number of employees.

On this day however, Naana assures the manager she can handle orders of hot chocolate drinks and hot caramel macchiato with the service and so the two drinks are included in the specials for the day.

Naana does a wonderful job on the day and the manager is impressed. At the end of the day, she receives good tips from the customers and beams with smiles as she hangs her apron after close of work.

Naana tells Toby how her day went during his absence. Toby is happy for Naana. She offers to share her tips with Toby as a form of appreciation for teaching her to make drinks like a professional barista. Toby refuses humbly, telling Naana he's happy to train her because she is passionate and willing to learn.

He tells her, "get ready for more recipes madam barista" as they share a laughter. Toby asks Naana to tell him one recipe she would love to learn and she happily responds, "**Cappuccino**".

## CAPPUCCINO

**Ingredients**
**:**
- **Espresso**
- **Milk**
- **Milk foam**
- **Cocoa poder (opt)**

**METHOD:**
- **In a mug/glass, pour 40ml espresso**
- **Add 40ml steamed milk**
- **Top up with milk foam**
- **Sprinkle a dust of cocoa powder**

Toby offers to include another recipe for Naana; **Vanilla Latte.**

**VANILLA LATTE:**

Ingredients:

- 1 cup Milk
- 40ml Espresso
- 10ml Vanilla syrup
- Ice
- Frothed milk (opt)

METHOD:
- In a glass, mix espresso and vanilla syrup
- Pour ice into a glass and add milk
- Pour your espresso mix into the Ice & milk
- Pour frothed milk on top

The days immediately after Toby's off day happens to be very busy days. As work closes, Toby offers one more recipe to Naana on paper and asks her to prepare it first thing in the morning for him to taste and remark.

**CAFFE MOCHA**

Ingredients:

- 5 ml Nut syrup of choice (opt)
- 30 ml Chocolate sauce
- 40 ml Espresso
- 1 cup Steamed milk

METHOD
- Mix nut syrup and chocolate sauce together
- Add the espresso and stir well
- Steam milk
- Pour steamed milk into a glass and add the espresso mix
- Sprinkle cocoa powder on surface

After a week of training and working, Naana is now a barista as she is able to take orders and prepare them to perfection. She is extremely happy about this. She decides to invite her friends over to the cafe soon.

When Naana tells her friends about her work at the cafe, one of them decides to have her birthday party celebration at the cafe. She inquires from Naana what drinks she could have for the occasion. Naana promises to revert.

Naana heads straight to the cafe to find out from Toby what drinks could be served for her friend's birthday party.
Toby offers to write a mocktail recipe for Naana to add to her rich knowledge of recipes.

## PINA COLADA

**Ingredients:**

- 100ml Pineapple juice
- 40ml Coconut puree
- 30ml Pina colada syrup
- 60ml full cream milk
- Ice cubes

**METHOD**
- Blend all ingredients together and serve

# JAMAICA

Ingredients:

- 50ml orange juice
- 50ml pineapple juice
- 30ml grenadine syrup
- Ice cubes

## METHOD
- Blend all ingredients and serve

# STRAWBERRY MOJITO

## Ingredients:

- 100ml Strawberry Puree
- 30ml Mojito mint syrup
- ¼ cup mint leaves
- 1 lemon
- 300ml soda water
- Ice cubes

## METHOD

- Blend all ingredients except the lemon
- Slice lemons and place in drink to serve

The birthday party goes very well. All of Naana's friends enjoy the drinks prepared by Naana so much that they promise to make Cafe Rouge their 'go-to' place for regular hang outs.

All too soon, the vacation season is over and Naana needs to go back to school. She has saved enough money to allow her to get the books she needs.

More importantly, Naana appreciates the skills she learned from Cafe Rouge, she is grateful to the manager for the opportunity and she is grateful to Toby for giving her a lifelong skill.

The contract between Naana and Cafe Rouge is executed. All obligations have been fulfilled by both parties and the contractual relationship has come to an end.